This joke book belongs to

Q. What kind of dog loves washing their hair?

A. A shampoodle.

Q. Why did the cow need a relaxing bath?

A. She was in need of some re-hoove-ination!

Q. Why did everyone want the mushroom to come to their party?

A. Because he was a fungi.

Knock knock
Who's there?
Great things
Great things who?
Great things come in spiny
packages!

Q. What do you call a bee who is a bad loser?

A. A cry ba-bee.

Q. Why did everyone want to be like the ice cream?

A. Because she was so cool.

Q. What do you get when you throw a chilli into the ocean?

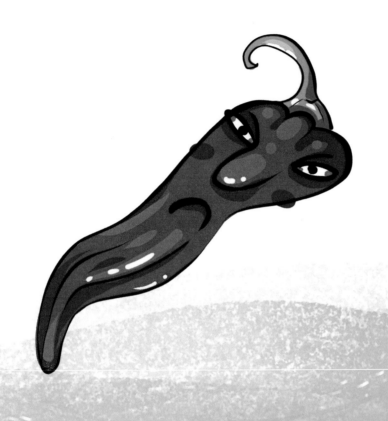

A. A heat wave.

Q. How do pigs talk to each other?

A. Swine language.

Q. What do you call a cow who drinks too much coffee in the morning?

A. Over Calfinated

Q. What new vegetable did Dad plant in the garden?

A. Beets me.

Q. What did one cactus say to another?

A. Looking sharp.

Q. Why shouldn't you start a business with a watermelon?

A. They're seedy.

Q. What do you call a bee who is unsure?

A. May-Bee

Q. Why is it hard to have a conversation when there is a goat nearby?

A. Because they are always butting in.

Q. Why did the pigeon cross the road?

A. It was the chickens day off.

Q. What kind of stores do dogs love?

A. Re-tail stores.

Q. Why was six scared
of seven?

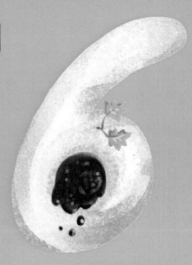

 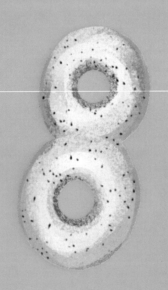 

A. Because 7 ate 9.

Q. What does an owl with an attitude most certainly have?

A. A scowl.

Q. Why did the unicorn fly across the road?

A. To meet her neigh-bours
on the other side.

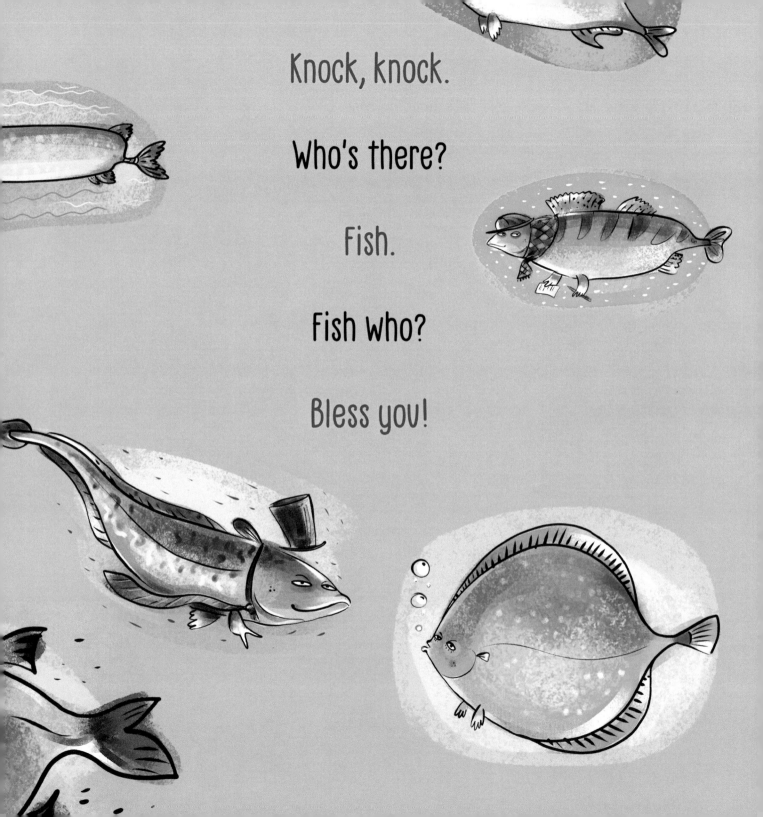

Knock, knock.

Who's there?

Fish.

Fish who?

Bless you!

Q. Why is it hard for leopards to hide?

A. Because they are always spotted.

Knock Knock

Who's there?

Bach

Bach who?

Bach bach I'm a chicken!

Made in United States
North Haven, CT
05 July 2022

20969455R00018